Catholic Christianity and Mental Health
Beliefs, Research and Applications

Harold G. Koenig, M.D.

ISBN:1544207646
ISBN-13: 978-1544207643

DEDICATION

To my Mother

CONTENTS

INTRODUCTION

The primary audience for this small book are mental health professionals and clergy who are called upon to help Catholics deal with emotional and other mental health problems. However, given the careful attention paid to documentation, researchers who conduct studies in Catholics and healthcare systems that provide services to Catholic patients will also find this extensively cited text useful. Finally, I think Catholics themselves will find the information contained here to be enlightening and help to deepen their Catholic faith. As someone with strong and long-standing Catholic roots, I have found my faith strengthened as I have done the research for this book. As a clinician and long-standing academic researcher, while acknowledging my personal biases, I have tried to be as objective as possible in presenting the material here and rigorously referencing it.

This book is the first in a series on Christianity and mental health in Catholics and Protestants. Since the historical development of Catholic Christianity occurred before Protestant Christianity, I begin this series by examining issues related to mental health in Catholics. In the second book of this series, I will examine Protestant Christianity and describe differences from Catholic Christianity and how this might affect the relationship with mental health among the faithful. However, there are many, many beliefs that unite Catholics and Protestants and mark them as "Christian," distinguishing them from other religious traditions. Most major Catholic and Protestant Christian denominations agree that Jesus is both human and divine, that he is God *incarnate* (in the flesh), both truly man and truly God.

The present volume will briefly trace Catholicism from its roots and describe how the faith tradition has evolved over time. Present day Catholic beliefs, practices, and values will then be succinctly summarized and their possible impact on mental health discussed (both positive and negative). Third, research on Catholic beliefs/practices and mental health in Catholics will be reviewed in order to identify the evidence base on which recommendations for mental health professionals and clergy will be grounded. Finally, clinical applications relevant to the treatment of Catholic clients and members of congregations based on the research evidence, clinical experience, and common sense will be recommended. After a brief summary and conclusions, the text will be followed by a list of references that have been cited therein.

Please join me on a journey that I think you will find enlightening for the mind and inspiring for the soul, as well as useful for professionals who care for the mental health needs of Catholics.

CHAPTER 1
HISTORICAL BACKGROUND

Strictly speaking, Catholic Christianity originated with the birth of Jesus of Nazareth. Both the Julian and Gregorian calendars, now used throughout much of the world, start with that event, with years marked as either BC or AD (BCE or CE in more neutral language). Bear in mind, however, that there are at least 40 calendars used throughout the world today, including the Chinese, Indian, Islamic, and Jewish calendars, each with their own start dates. Regarding the Gregorian calendar, AD stands for Anno Domini ("in the year of the Lord") and BC stands for Before Christ. Catholicism, then, began at time 0 on the Gregorian calendar.

The Catholic Church, however, did not have its true start until the beginning of Jesus' ministry in 30 AD based on Luke 3:23: "When he began, Jesus was about thirty years old"[1] (assuming here that Jesus was a real historical person). It would probably be more accurate to say that the Catholic *Church* actually began when Christians began meeting together in various places during the 1st century AD. The earliest use of the term "Catholic Church" is from

---

[1] All quotations are from New Jerusalem Bible (NJB), the Catholic translation (from Hebrew, Greek or Aramaic) of the Bible published in 1985 by Doubleday (New York, NY)

a letter written by the early church father Ignatius to Christians in Smyrna around 106 AD: "Wherever the bishop shall appear, there let the multitude [of the people] also be; even as, wherever Jesus Christ is, there is the Catholic Church" (Strawley, 1900). Later, St. Cyril (circa 315-386) is quoted as saying: "If ever thou art sojourning in cities, inquire not simply where the Lord's House is, nor merely where the Church is, but where is the Catholic Church. For this is the peculiar name of this Holy Church, the mother of us all, which is the spouse of our Lord Jesus Christ, the Only-begotten Son of God" (cited in Berry, 2009, p 68).

With regard to the institutional leadership, it was not until the end of the 2nd century that bishops (successors to Jesus's 12 disciples) began congregating in regional meetings to discuss and resolve doctrinal issues. In the 3rd century, the leading bishop (Bishop of Rome) began to have meetings to discuss problems that the other bishops could not resolve on their own. The Catholic pope is considered the Bishop of Rome and is believed by Catholics to be the direct successor of Saint Peter, one of Jesus' disciples about whom he said "You are Peter and on this rock I will build my community" (Mathew 16:18). In 380 AD, the Roman Emperor decreed Christianity to be the official religion of the Roman Empire. After the fall of the Western Roman Empire in 476 AD, the Church began to establish monasteries and send missionaries throughout Northern Europe and the British Isles (Norman & Barrett, 2007).

In the 7th century AD, the Eastern Catholic Church came under invasion by Islam, which by the middle of the 8th century had destroyed three of the five major Catholic centers (called "patriarchal sees") located in Jerusalem (Israel), Alexandria (Egypt), and Antioch (Turkey). Over the next several centuries, the Catholic Church and Islam fought for control of various regions in the East and the West, including Rome itself, which was sacked in 850 AD. Constantinople in the East was also besieged during this time by Islam, although the Christian faith was preserved. By the 11th century, friction began to develop between the Latin Western Church and the largely Greek Eastern Church, and in 1054 AD, the Eastern Orthodox Church split off from the Roman Catholic Church (called the East-West Schism or "Great Schism").

The Eastern Orthodox Church (or simply Orthodox) should be distinguished from the 22 Eastern Catholic Churches (Ukrainian,

Greek, Greek Melkite, Maronite, Byzantine Ruthenian, Coptic Catholic, Syro Malabar, Syro-Malankara, Chaldean, Ethiopic Rites), which consider themselves Catholic but not *Roman* Catholic (Roman Catholic also called the "Latin Rite").

In the 16th century, Protestant reformers (Martin Luther, John Calvin, and others) started to challenge the doctrine and practices of the Roman Catholic Church, creating the second major split. In response, the Church began a series of reforms that would later be called the "Catholic-Reformation" or "Catholic Revival" beginning with the Council of Trent (1545 AD). However, this was not enough for the Protestant reformers in Europe who gradually began to win over the people of the region (especially northern Europe and the British Isles). As its base in Europe began to erode, however, the Roman Catholic Church would spread widely around the world especially to the Americas (in particular, Mexico, Central America, and South America).

Catholicism Today

The Roman Catholic Church is the oldest and largest Christian organization in the world with a membership of nearly 1.3 billion (Annuarium Statisticum Ecclesiae, 2016). In comparison, the Eastern Orthodox Church has a membership of approximately 200 million (Fairchild, 2016) and the Protestant churches approximately 800 million. The major differences between the Catholic and Orthodox Churches involve the primacy of the Catholic pope's leadership, a disagreement about the wording of the Nicene Creed (concerning the doctrine of the Trinity), and belief regarding the purification of those who have died (i.e., purgatory). Otherwise, there is general agreement between the two confessions (Ut Unum, 1995). In the United States, one in five adults (21% or 68 million) is Roman Catholic (Pew Research Center, 2016), although that percentage appears to be changing.

In 2014, the Pew Research Center's Religious Landscape Study found that while 32% of Americans reported they were raised Catholic, 41% no longer identified themselves as Catholic (Pew Research Center, 2015a). Based on those figures, 13% of Americans are former Catholics, 19% of Americans were raised Catholic and currently identify as Catholic, and 2% of Americans have converted to Catholicism. The recent scandal involving child abuse by priests may have had something to do with the changing Catholic landscape. The scandal received enormous public attention (both the perpetration and the cover up). The absolute prevalence of child abuse in priests has been estimated to be about 4% (USCCB, 2004) and up to 7% in some part of the world (Wright & Roberts, 2017), although bear in mind that the latter figure is for priests "accused of abuse," not cases of abuse that have been documented and confirmed. Compare these rates to 10% of the non-clergy adult male population that is involved in pedophilia (Awad & Saunders, 1991). While this means 96% of Catholic priests have not been involved in child abuse and the rate of abuse by priests is less than half of that by males more generally, the fact that such abuses have occurred at all by these trusted clergy has likely adversely affected the faith of many Catholics.

CHAPTER 2
BASIC CATHOLIC BELIEFS

Almost all Christian denominations[1] (particularly Catholic and Protestant) agree on the basic beliefs described in the Nicene Creed established in 325 AD at the First Council of Nicaea in present day Iznik, Turkey, and amended in 381 AD at the First Council of Constantinople in present day Istanbul (**Table 1**). The Nicene Creed affirms the divinity of Jesus, i.e., the "co-essential divinity of the Son" and his pre-existence as the Word of God.

Catholics, then, believe in the Divinity of Jesus Christ and in the Trinity, i.e., one and the same God in three persons -- the Father, the Son, and the Holy Spirit (81% of all U.S. Catholics and 97% of weekly Mass attendees say they have no doubt about this) (CARA, 2008). Catholicism is considered a monotheistic faith tradition, a tradition whose members believe in one (and only one) God. The beliefs of Catholics are described by the *Catechism of the Catholic Church*, which was approved by Pope John Paul II in 1992. The core beliefs of Catholics are indeed those contained in the Nicene Creed.[2]

---

[1] Note that there are also "nontrinitarian" denominations within Christianity that do not strictly follow the Nicene Creed, include Mormons (Church of Jesus Christ of Latter-day Saints) and Jehovah's Witnesses.

[2] What we believe. *United States Conference of Catholic Bishops*. Retrieved from http://www.usccb.org/beliefs-and-teachings/what-we-believe/ (accessed on 1/6/17)

Table 1. The Nicene Creed [1]

We believe in one God, the Father, the Almighty, maker of heaven and earth, of all that is seen and unseen.

We believe in one Lord, Jesus Christ, the only Son of God, eternally begotten of the Father, God from God, Light from Light, true God from true God, begotten, not made, one in Being with the Father.

Through him all things were made. For us men and for our salvation he came down from heaven: by the power of the Holy Spirit he was born of the Virgin Mary, and became man.

For our sake he was crucified under Pontius Pilate; he suffered, died, and was buried.

On the third day he rose again in fulfillment of the Scriptures; he ascended into heaven and is seated on the right hand of the Father.

He will come again in glory to judge the living and the dead, and his kingdom will have no end.

We believe in the Holy Spirit, the Lord, the giver of life, who proceeds from the Father and the Son. With the Father and the Son he is worshipped and glorified. He has spoken through the Prophets.

We believe in one holy catholic and apostolic Church.

We acknowledge one baptism for the forgiveness of sins.

We look for the resurrection of the dead, and the life of the world to come. Amen.

---

[1] Nicene Creed. Encyclopædia Britannica. Retrieved on from https://www.britannica.com/topic/Nicene-Creed (accessed on 1/18/17)

God

The Catechism of the Catholic Church (CCC) (1993) says: "Our profession of faith begins with *God*, for God is the First and the Last, the beginning and the end of everything. The Credo begins with God the *Father*, for the Father is the first divine person of the Most Holy Trinity; our Creed begins with the creation of heaven and earth, for creation is the beginning and the foundation of all God's works" (CCC Part 1, Section 2, Chapter 1:198).   Catholics believe that humans are made in God's image and likeness. Catholics also believe in the 10 Commandments, including the 1st Commandment: "'I am Yahweh your God who brought you out of Egypt, where you lived as slaves. You shall have no other gods to rival me" (Exodus 20:2-3). Catholics believe in the two Great Commandments given by Jesus Christ in Matthew 22:37, the first one being: "You must love the Lord your God with all your heart, with all your soul, and with all your mind."

Jesus

Catholics believe that Jesus Christ is the "Son of God," the second person of the Trinity, fully God and fully human (CCC Part 1, Section 2, Chapter 2:430-455). He is the only mediator between God and man (however, as members of the Body of Christ, Christians are allowed to share in that mediation). Jesus is the fullness of God's revelation, the Messiah, and the savior of the world. As both human and God, he has saved humans from their sin and separation from God through his suffering, death and resurrection (as the Creed indicates).

Salvation (justification)

Catholics believe that humans must know, love, and serve God through Jesus Christ in this world in order to obtain the happiness of heaven in the next. The Catholic Catechism says: "The grace of the Holy Spirit has the power to justify us, that is, to cleanse us from our sins and to communicate to us 'the righteousness of God through faith in Jesus Christ' and through Baptism" (CCC Part 3, Section 1, Chapter 3:1987). Salvation is by grace only, a free gift from God. However, one receives God's grace gradually through participation in the Catholic Church. Catholics believe that people are "saved" by faith <u>and</u> by works, not by one or the other alone. Catholics believe that salvation is a process that occurs over time as one is involved in the life of the Catholic Church (the "repository of saving grace"). In Catholicism, "salvation" and "sanctification" are merged into one and the same process. Protestants, in contrast, separate the terms: salvation is conferred immediately by what Jesus Christ has done when a person confesses Jesus as savior and enters into the Christian life, whereas sanctification is the slow process whereby a person conforms her or his life to the teachings of the Christian faith.

Purgatory

Because salvation and sanctification (the process of being purified of one's sins) are necessary in order to enter heaven, Catholics believe that there is an intermediate place (a state of suffering between heaven and hell) called Purgatory, where people ultimately destined for heaven must pass through after they die. The Catholic Catechism says: "All who die in God's grace and friendship, but still imperfectly purified, are indeed assured of their eternal salvation; but after death they undergo purification, so as to achieve the holiness necessary to enter the joy of heaven" (CCC Part 1, Section 2, Chapter 3:1030). Purgatory is where humans can work through any remaining sins, become purified and be made ready for heaven. Protestants, in contrast to Catholics, believe that Jesus Christ died for all people's sins, making them holy and faultless before God, therefore not requiring Purgatory. In his writings, Pope John Paul II approaches the Protestant view by emphasizing the role that Jesus Christ plays in that purification. He said "the term purgatory does not indicate a place, but a condition of existence," where Christ "removes ... the remnants of imperfection" (John Paul II, 1999).

Heaven and Hell

The Catholic Catechism says: "Those who die in God's grace and friendship and are perfectly purified live forever with Christ. They are like God for ever, for they 'see him as he is,' face to face. This perfect life with the Most Holy Trinity - this communion of life and love with the Trinity, with the Virgin Mary, the angels and all the blessed - is called 'heaven.' Heaven is the ultimate end and fulfillment of the deepest human longings, the state of supreme, definitive happiness. To live in heaven is 'to be with Christ'" (CCC Part 1, Section 2, Chapter 3:1023-1025). Among U.S. Catholics, three-quarters (76%) say they have no doubt that "There is a Heaven" (CARA, 2008).

The Catholic Catechism also says: "We cannot be united with God unless we freely choose to love him. But we cannot love God if we sin gravely against him, against our neighbor or against ourselves: 'He who does not love remains in death. Anyone who hates his brother is a murderer, and you know that no murderer has eternal life abiding in him' [citing 1 John 3:14]. Our Lord warns us that we shall be separated from him if we fail to meet the serious needs of the poor and the little ones who are his brethren. To die in mortal sin without repenting and accepting God's merciful love means remaining separated from him forever by our own free choice. This state of definitive self-exclusion from communion with God and the blessed is called 'hell'" (CCC Part 1, Section 2, Chapter 3:1033). Two-thirds of U.S. Catholics (67%) indicate that they have no doubt that "There is a Hell" (78% of weekly Mass attendees) (CARA, 2008).

The Bible

Catholics believe that God revealed himself in the Bible, all 46 books of the Hebrew Bible and all 27 books of the New Testament. This was the original Bible (canon agreed on in 367 AD) and remained so until the 16th century. After the Protestant Reformation, Protestants dropped 7 books from the original Bible to form the Protestant Bible. The "rule of faith" among Catholics is based on both what is contained in the Bible and in "sacred tradition" (not the Bible alone, i.e., *Sola Scriptura*, as Protestants believe). For Catholics, sacred tradition is valued equally in reverence and devotion as the Bible. From 40 to 65 years after Jesus' death, the New Testament was transmitted orally by word of mouth (Robinson, 2000; Geisler, 1998; Mounce, 1998). This is similar to what Catholics mean by the term 'sacred tradition.' Catholics interpret the Bible in a "literal" sense: "the meaning conveyed by the words of Scripture and discovered by exegesis, following the rules of sound interpretation" (CCC Part 1, Section 1, Chapter 2:116). This is different than the "literalist" interpretation, which maintains that whatever a passage of Scripture says is what it means (in other words, if the Bible said the world was created in six days then it was created in 144 hours).

Mary and the Saints

The Catholic Catechism says: "'The Virgin Mary. . . is acknowledged and honored as being truly the Mother of God and of the redeemer. . . . She is 'clearly the mother of the members of Christ'. . . (963) since she has by her charity joined in bringing about the birth of believers in the Church, who are members of its head. 'Mary, Mother of Christ, Mother of the Church'...By her complete adherence to the Father's will, to his Son's redemptive work, and to every prompting of the Holy Spirit, the Virgin Mary is the Church's model of faith and charity. Thus she is a 'preeminent and. . . wholly unique member of the Church'; indeed, she is the 'exemplary realization' of the Church" (967) (CCC Part 1, Section 2, Chapter 3).

Thus, Mary, as the mother of God, has a special place in Catholic belief. Catholics believe it is appropriate to pray *through* (not to) Mary or *through* the Saints who are viewed as holy people who intercede between humans and God. Mary and the Saints are not worshiped themselves, but are honored and venerated, viewed as role models, and considered intercessors. This is similar to a person asking friends and family to pray (or intercede) for him or her. Among U.S. Catholics, 73% have no doubt that "Mary, the Mother of God, was immaculately conceived without original sin" (90% of weekly Mass attendees) (CARA, 2008).

The Church

Catholics believe that the Catholic Church is the only church today that can make the claim that it was founded 2000 years ago by Jesus Christ himself; all other churches have been founded by other individuals at later dates. The Catholic Catechism says: "'This is the sole Church of Christ, which in the Creed we profess to be one, holy, catholic and apostolic.' These four characteristics, inseparably linked with each other, indicate essential features of the Church and her mission. The Church does not possess them of herself; it is Christ who, through the Holy Spirit, makes his Church one, holy, catholic, and apostolic, and it is he who calls her to realize each of these qualities" (CCC Part 1, Section 2, Chapter 3:811). Catholics believe that Jesus teaches people how to know, love and serve God *through the Catholic Church*.

The Pope

The authority structure of the Catholic Church is vertical, in contrast to the horizontal structure of most Protestant churches, which profess the "priesthood of all believers." Catholics believe in the sovereign authority of the Pope (the Bishop of Rome) over all members of the church. The Pope acts through bishops, archbishops, and cardinals. Cardinals are bishops selected by the Pope who form the College of Cardinals. They also elect the next Pope and make other important church decisions. Bishops are in charge of local dioceses, and archbishops are in charge of really large local dioceses. A diocese is made up of local parishes (a parish is usually covered by a specific Catholic church), which are led by parish priests. Other Catholic clergy include monks, deacons, and nuns/sisters (the only female Catholic clergy).

Summary

These are the primary tenets of the Catholic faith. Of course, not all Catholics believe everything above and there is a range of belief even among Catholic clergy in this regard. Nevertheless, these beliefs are generally considered core Catholic beliefs that the majority of Catholics ascribe to.

CHAPTER 3
CATHOLIC PRACTICES

Catholic beliefs are expressed on a day-to-day basis through Catholic practices. The seven Sacraments describe some of the most important of these practices.

The Sacraments

The Catholic Catechism says: "The whole liturgical life of the Church revolves around the Eucharistic sacrifice and the sacraments. There are seven sacraments in the Church: Baptism, Confirmation or Chrismation, Eucharist, Penance, Anointing of the Sick, Holy Orders, and Matrimony" (CCC Part 2, Section 1, Chapter 1:1113). The sacraments were codified at the Council of Trent (1545-1563 AD). The Catholic Catechism also says "The sacraments are efficacious signs of grace, instituted by Christ and entrusted to the Church, by which divine life is dispensed to us. The visible rites by which the sacraments are celebrated signify and make present the graces proper to each sacrament. They bear fruit in those who receive them with the required dispositions" (CCC Part 2, Section 1, Chapter 1:1131).

Given that salvation is conferred by grace through the life of the Catholic Church, participation in the sacraments is essential for the receipt of that grace. Four of the above sacraments (baptism, confirmation, Eucharist, and penance/confession) are meant for all Catholics, and are necessary for initiation into the Catholic faith. The remaining three sacraments are specific to the individual and the situation (anointing of the sick, matrimony, and holy orders).

1. Baptism. Catholics believe that infant baptism is necessary because of "original sin" and is not symbolic. Rather, baptism (as an infant or as an adult) directly "saves" a person, makes him/her a member of the Body of Christ, washes away sin, and conveys the Holy Spirit to that person (CCC Part 2, Section 2, Chapter 1:1213-1284). Baptism is performed only once.

2. Confirmation. The conferring of the sacrament of confirmation usually takes place in early adolescence (around the age of 14, and after baptism). This is a way that Catholics at an age of accountability can confirm their faith commitment and begin to equip themselves with the seven gifts of the Holy Spirit: wisdom, understanding, right judgment, courage, knowledge, reverence, and wonder or awe (CCC Part 2, Section 2, Chapter 1:1303). These gifts are used to serve as a witness to their faith in Jesus Christ, through "thought, word, and deed" (Lumen Gentium, 1964). Catholics believe that they are to be the presence of Jesus in the world in order to bring all people to God. Like baptism, confirmation is performed only once. While 95% of Catholics born pre-Vatican II (before 1962) was confirmed, only 69% of the Millennial Generation (born 1980 to 2000) has received this sacrament (CARA, 2008).

3. Eucharist. The Eucharist is very important to Catholics, who are expected to receive the wafer (body of Christ) and drink the wine (blood of Christ) during "the Mass" (the name for Catholic Church services). However, if the person has committed any serious sins, he or she is encouraged to first go to confession (below) before taking the Eucharist. Catholics believe that Jesus Christ is literally (not symbolically) present in the Holy Eucharist, including all of him -- his body and blood, as well as his divinity (called "Doctrine of the Real Presence" or transubstantiation) (CCC Part 2, Section 2, Chapter 1:1374). Youth usually receive this sacrament for the first time around the age of 7 or 8 years (called First Holy Communion). The Eucharist is offered at every Mass, and all baptized Catholics are encouraged to receive it at that time (only baptized Catholics and only those without an unconfessed "grave" sin). Although many Catholics receive it weekly or even daily, the Eucharist cannot be

taken more than two times per day (according to Canon Law). The Pew Research Center (2015b) found that 43% of U.S. Catholics receive the Eucharist every time they attend Mass; among Catholics who have received their First Holy Communion and attend Mass at least once/week, the figure is 79% (CARA, 2008).

4. <u>Penance</u> (confession). Catholics believe that they should confess grave or "mortal" sins to a priest (sacrament of confession), but can go directly to God to confess minor sins (as Jesus instructed in the Lord's Prayer, Matthew 6:9-13) (CCC Part 2, Section 2, Chapter 2: 1446-1447). Confession usually takes place in a small cubicle where the person confesses sins and the priest absolves them and gives the person "penance" to do (penance involves actions to make up for the sins, such as saying a certain number of prayers or doing good deeds). There is no light in the confession booth, and the person is separated from the priest by a screen (making it completely anonymous). Many Catholics go to confession regularly to confess their minor sins, even if they haven't committed a mortal sin. A mortal sin, however, is a serious one that blocks a person's relationship with God and may prevent the person from going to heaven unless they confess and have it absolved by a priest. Confession is required only after committing a mortal sin; however, Catholics are encouraged to go once a month. Approximately 2% of U.S. Catholics go once/month, 30% go about once/year, and 45% never go (CARA, 2008).

5. <u>Anointing of the Sick</u> (also called unction or extreme unction). This sacrament is administered by an ordained priest or bishop to a person who has attained the age of reason and is sick. The anointing is with oil that has been blessed for this purpose. Although the sacrament in the past was usually administered only to those who were dying and just before death ("last rites"), it is now given to anyone who is seriously ill or really old (even when not dying) if requested (CCC Part 2, Section 2, Chapter 2: 1514-1515). Although this sacrament is usually only administered to those with serious physical illness, it may also be administered to those with serious mental illness (based on the logic that many mental illnesses are physical diseases of the brain) (Zenit, 2010). The sacrament is intended to provide peace and courage, renew trust and faith in God, strengthen the person against the temptation to become discouraged

or disheartened, and even provide forgiveness of sins if the person is unconscious or unable to confess (CCC Part 2, Section 2, Chapter 2:1520). The sacrament is usually administered following confession and receiving the Eucharist. It can be repeated if the person recovers and then falls ill again, although a frequency of once/month would likely be too often. About half (51%) of U.S. Catholics have requested this sacrament for themselves or a sick family member (CARA, 2008).

6.   Matrimony.   For Catholics, marriage is a holy sacrament performed for life ("for richer or poorer, in sickness or in health until death do you part") and cannot be broken prior to the death of one partner except in rare cases (CCC Part 3, Section 2, Chapter 2:2382). Today, the priest may "annul" a marriage depending on the particular circumstances of the couple, although there is usually a rather lengthy process that must be gone through to determine if there are grounds for annulment (decided on by the priest). If a Catholic remarries before the original marriage has been annulled, then excommunication from the church is the result. Pope Francis recently streamlined the process by which divorced Catholics can get an annulment from the Catholic Church (in just 45 days if both members of the couple agree), although this prompted the "no sex" rule by Catholic Church leaders, which means that divorced Catholics can get remarried but cannot have sex until the annulment of the original marriage is final (Doughty, 2015).

7. Holy Orders. This sacrament qualifies Catholic priests to serve in the Catholic Church, and is conferred by a Catholic bishop. Considerable training, including a bachelor's and master's degree from a Catholic seminary or graduate school is usually required for ordination into the priesthood. A vow of celibacy accompanies this sacrament, and the sacrament is only administered to men (CCC Part 2, Section 2, Chapter 3:1538, 1577, 1579). Approximately one in six (16%) Catholic men have considered becoming a priest or a religious brother (CARA, 2008).

Other Catholic Practices

Besides participating in the life of the Catholic Church through the sacraments, there are many other Catholic practices as well.

Attending Religious Services. Catholics are obligated to attend Mass (religious service) once a week on Sunday, based on the 3rd Commandment in Exodus 20:8: "Remember the Sabbath day and keep it holy." Approximately one-third of U.S. Catholics (31.4%) attend Mass on any given week (CARA, 2008).

Prayer. Catholics believe in prayer before meals, bedtime, and at other times as well. Pew Research Center (2014) indicates that 59% of Catholics pray daily.

Saying the Rosary. "Saying" (praying) the rosary is a practice that many Catholics engage in, particularly women. The rosary is a string with a cross followed by five groups of ten small beads (decade), with additional large beads before each decade. Saying the rosary means saying the Lord's Prayer (large bead) followed by a set of 10 Hail Mary's (small beads), which for the full rosary is repeated five times. Approximately half of Catholics (52%) report that they say the rosary (CARA, 2008).

Fasting and Abstinence. The United States Conference of Bishops (2017) declares the following: "Ash Wednesday and Good Friday are obligatory days of fasting and abstinence for Catholics. In addition, Fridays during Lent are obligatory days of abstinence. For members of the Latin Catholic Church, the norms on fasting are obligatory from age 18 until age 59. When fasting, a person is permitted to eat one full meal, as well as two smaller meals that together are not equal to a full meal. The norms concerning abstinence from meat are binding upon members of the Latin Catholic Church from age 14 onwards." Among U.S. Catholics, about 60% say they abstain from meat on all Fridays during Lent (CARA, 2008).

Donating Money or Time. Two-thirds of U.S. Catholics (62%) report that working to help the poor and needy is essential to being "Catholic" (Pew Research Center, 2015c). Catholics are not obligated to tithe a certain percentage of their income to the Catholic Church. However, the Catholic Catechism says: "The fifth precept ('You shall help to provide for the needs of the Church') means that the faithful are obliged to assist with the material needs of the Church, each according to his own ability. The faithful also have the duty of providing for the material needs of the Church, each according to his own abilities" (CCC Part 3, Section 1, Chapter 3:2043). The Code of Cannon Law (1983) also says: "The Christian faithful are obliged to assist with the needs of the Church so that the Church has what is necessary for divine worship, for the works of the apostolate and of charity, and for the decent support of ministers. They are also obliged to promote social justice and, mindful of the precept of the Lord, to assist the poor from their own resources." The Catholic Church is one of the largest charitable organizations in the world, and in the United States alone, the total revenue taken in for charitable purposes by Catholic Charities and Catholic Relief Services combined equaled $1.29 billion (making these two charities combined the 5th largest U.S. charity) according to *Forbes Magazine* (Barrett, 2016). Among working-age U.S. Catholics, 45% are members of a household that regularly gives weekly to their parish (92% of weekly Mass attendees) (Gray et al., 2013). Approximately one-third (34%) give $100 or less per year, one-third (33%) give $101-505 per year, and one-third (33%) give $501 or more per year (48% of weekly Mass attendees give $501 or more per year). Also, see Indulgences below.

Observing Holy Days. In addition to Sundays, the obligatory Holy Days in the U.S. during the year are the Solemnity of Mary (Jan 1), Ascension of Jesus (May 5), Assumption of the Blessed Virgin Mary (August 15), All Saints Day (November 1), Feast of Immaculate Conception (December 8), and Christmas (December 25). Catholics are obligated to attend Mass on Holy Days. Lent (40 days before Easter) is an important time for Catholics, especially the week before Easter. As noted above, about 60% of U.S. Catholics say they abstain from meat on Lenten Fridays, and 45% say they typically attend and receive ashes at the Ash Wednesday church service (at the start of Lent) (CARA, 2008).

Miscellaneous Practices. Common religious practices of Catholics include lighting candles for loved ones (alive and deceased), wearing or carrying a crucifix or cross (32% of all Catholics and 39% of those who attend Mass weekly), wearing or carrying a medal or pin of an angel or saint such as St Christopher or St Francis of Assisi (42% of Catholics who attend weekly Mass), and having a picture or statue of Mary on display in their homes (59% of all Catholics, 67% of Hispanics, and 80% of those who attend Mass weekly) (CARA, 2008).

Indulgences

There is much misinformation and confusion with regard to this particular Catholic practice. Some Catholics and many non-Catholics believe that an indulgence is giving money to the Church to pay off sins and thereby reduces the time spent in Purgatory. Even if this were true, attempts by Catholic clergy to obtain donations to the Church for this reason would not be all that different than what happens in many Protestant churches today. In order to increase Sunday offerings, many Protestant pastors promise the faithful blessings in heaven for giving generously (see Warren, 2002, p 34).

The abuse of this practice in the Catholic Church, however, was one reason why Martin Luther ignited the Protestant Reformation in 1517. While the selling of indulgences ("paying off of sins") was common by some unscrupulous priests during the Middle Ages, the Catholic Church outlawed the practice in 1567, calling it "simony" (after Simon the magician who tried to buy the Holy Spirit from Peter, see Act 8:9-24). Simony is defined by the Catholic Catechism as "the buying or selling of spiritual things" (CCC Part 3, Section 2, Chapter 1:2121). The Catholic Catechism defines an indulgence as "a remission before God of the temporal punishment due to sins whose guilt has already been forgiven, which the faithful Christian who is duly disposed gains under certain prescribed conditions through the action of the Church which, as the minister of redemption, dispenses and applies with authority the treasury of the satisfactions of Christ and the saints" (CCC Part 2, Section 2, Chapter 2:1471). The "treasury" here refers to the one in heaven based on Matthew 6:19 "Do not store up treasures for yourselves on earth, where moth and woodworm destroy them and thieves can break in and steal. But store up treasures for yourselves in heaven, where neither moth nor woodworm destroys them and thieves cannot break in and steal." In Catholicism today, an indulgence usually means saying a particular prayer, visiting a particular place, or performing specific good works.

CHAPTER 4
CATHOLIC VALUES

Catholic ethics and values reflect the beliefs and practices of Catholics. The ten primary Catholic values are: respect for human life, respect for human dignity, respect for creation, justice, love and compassion, service, forgiveness, peace, faithfulness, and integrity (adapted from Catholic Catechist, 2016). These values are described briefly below. Since respect for human life is one of the most important values to Catholics, more attention is paid to its description here.

Respect for Human Life

Catholics believe that men and women are created in God's image. Therefore, human life is considered precious and sacred in all its forms from embryo to advanced old age, regardless of whether a person is healthy, sick, or disabled. From this belief come the Catholic teachings concerning abortion, physician-assisted suicide or euthanasia, and suicide.

Abortion. The Catholic Catechism states: "Human life must be respected and protected absolutely from the moment of conception. From the first moment of his existence, a human being must be recognized as having the rights of a person - among which is the inviolable right of every innocent being to life. Since the first century the Church has affirmed the moral evil of every procured abortion. This teaching has not changed and remains unchangeable. Direct abortion, that is to say, abortion willed either as an end or a means, is gravely contrary to the moral law. Formal cooperation in an abortion constitutes a grave offense. The Church attaches the canonical penalty of excommunication to this crime against human life. 'A person who procures a completed abortion incurs excommunication latae sententiae,' 'by the very commission of the offense...'" (CCC Part 3, Section 2, Chapter 2:2270-2272).

These views, says the Catholic Catechism, are based on the following three Biblical scriptures:

"Before I formed you in the womb I knew you; before you came to birth I consecrated you" (Jeremiah 1:5)

"My frame was not hidden from you, when I was being made in secret, intricately wrought in the depths of the earth" (Psalm 22:10-11)

"For so many marvels I thank you; a wonder am I, and all your works are wonders. You knew me through and through, my being held no secrets from you, when I was being formed in secret, textured in the depths of the earth. Your eyes could see my embryo. In your book all my days were inscribed, every one that was fixed is there" (Psalm 139:14-16)

<u>Physician-Assisted Suicide or Euthanasia</u>. The Catechism is also clear in stating: "Those whose lives are diminished or weakened deserve special respect. Sick or handicapped persons should be helped to lead lives as normal as possible. Whatever its motives and means, direct euthanasia consists in putting an end to the lives of handicapped, sick, or dying persons. It is morally unacceptable" (CCC Part 3, Section 2, Chapter 2:2276-2277). Elsewhere, the Catechism states: "Voluntary co-operation in suicide [for physicians] is contrary to the moral law" (CCC Part 3, Section 2, Chapter 2:2282).

<u>Suicide</u>. With regard to taking one's own life by suicide, the Catechism states: "Everyone is responsible for his life before God who has given it to him. It is God who remains the sovereign Master of life. We are obliged to accept life gratefully and preserve it for his honor and the salvation of our souls. We are stewards, not owners, of the life God has entrusted to us. It is not ours to dispose of...

Suicide is contrary to love for the living God. If suicide is committed with the intention of setting an example, especially to the young, it also takes on the gravity of scandal" (CCC Part 3, Section 2, Chapter 2:2280-2282).

Until recent times the decision to end one's life was considered a "mortal sin" that forever condemned the person to hell (in part, because the person was unable to confess the sin and receive absolution for it before death) (Makinen, 2014). Believing that suicide may separate a person from loved ones for all eternity was a powerful belief that kept Catholics from committing suicide (as Emile Durkheim, the founder of modern sociology, observed in 1897). Many family members of those who died from suicide, then, grieved heavily since there was no possibility of their seeing the loved one ever again. However, the latest version of the Catechism has made mental illness an exception to this earlier rule that promises eternal damnation, instead leaving it up to God: "Grave psychological disturbances, anguish, or grave fear of hardship, suffering, or torture can diminish the responsibility of the one committing suicide. We should not despair of the eternal salvation of persons who have taken their own lives. By ways known to him alone, God can provide the opportunity for salutary repentance. The Church prays for persons who have taken their own lives" (CCC Part 3, Section 2, Chapter 2:2282-2283).

Respect for Human Dignity

This value, related to respect for human life, includes the belief that all people are unique, have something to offer, and have infinite worth and value to the Creator (CCC Part 2, Section 1, Chapter 1). This leads to efforts to defend human rights wherever they are being violated.

Respect for Creation

Catholics value the natural world's beauty and feel responsible for being a good steward of this beauty, which is under their care. Thus, Catholics advocate for initiatives that preserve the environment for future generations, rather than destroy it. The Catechism says: "The seventh commandment enjoins respect for the integrity of creation. Animals, like plants and inanimate beings, are by nature destined for the common good of past, present, and future humanity. Use of the mineral, vegetable, and animal resources of the universe cannot be divorced from respect for moral imperatives. Man's dominion over inanimate and other living beings granted by the Creator is not absolute; it is limited by concern for the quality of life of his neighbor, including generations to come; it requires a religious respect for the integrity of creation." (CCC Part 3, Section 2, Chapter 2:2415)

Justice

Justice is one of the four "cardinal" virtues that Catholics believe are pivotal and around which all other virtues are grouped (temperance, prudence, justice, courage). The Catechism says: "*Justice* is the moral virtue that consists in the constant and firm will to give their due to God and neighbor. Justice toward God is called the 'virtue of religion.' Justice toward men disposes one to respect the rights of each and to establish in human relationships the harmony that promotes equity with regard to persons and to the common good. The just man, often mentioned in the Sacred Scriptures, is distinguished by habitual right thinking and the uprightness of his conduct toward his neighbor. 'You shall not be partial to the poor or defer to the great, but in righteousness shall you judge your neighbor.' 'Masters, treat your slaves justly and fairly, knowing that you also have a Master in heaven'" (CCC Part 3, Section 1, Chapter 1:1807). Justice includes following the laws of the state and governing authorities (based on Romans 13:1-5, Titus 3:1, 1 Peter 2:13-17).

Love and Compassion

Following the second Great Commandment, Catholics believe that they should love others: "You must love your neighbour as yourself" (Matthew 22:39). According to John 13:34-35, when Catholics show love like this they let others know that they are followers of Jesus. Jesus raises the bar even further by telling his followers that they are to love their enemies and those who hurt them (Luke 6:27-32). Showing respect, compassion, and sensitivity to the needy, then, is one way that Catholics show that they are followers of Jesus. Catholics believe that this principle is illustrated in the parable of the Good Samaritan (Luke 10:29-37), when after saying that people must love their neighbor as themselves, Jesus is asked by an expert in the

Jewish law the following question: "who is my neighbour?" His answer was basically the following: any person in need of help, regardless of religion or ethnic background. The Catechism says: "Love is the fundamental and innate vocation of every human being" (CCC Part 3, Section 2, Chapter 2:2392).

Service

Catholics believe that the vocation to love and show compassion will require that they serve one another by feeding the hungry, providing clothe for those who cannot afford them, and providing shelter for those who are without (following Jesus' imperative in Matthew 25:35-36). This is one reason why Catholic Charities has a division called Catholic Social Services (CSS 2016), which provides "basic and emergency needs, homelessness, immigration issues, housing and residential services, disabilities, adoption, mental health counseling, elder health services, neighborhood rehabilitation, foreclosure help, citizenship services" to needy people and to low income families. CSS is one of the largest social service providers in the United States and Caritas International is one of the largest service organizations in the world (serving more than 200 countries or territories).

Forgiveness

Catholics believe in forgiveness of others because of what Jesus said in many places in the Gospels, particularly in the Lord's Prayer: "forgive us our debts, as we have forgiven those who are in debt to us" (Mathew 6:12). Unless they forgive others, Catholics believe that God will not forgive them. Catholics also hold to Jesus' teaching that holding a grudge is not compatible with being one of his followers, indicating in Luke 6:29-31: "To anyone who slaps you on one cheek, present the other cheek as well; to anyone who takes your cloak from you, do not refuse your tunic. Give to everyone who asks you, and do not ask for your property back from someone who takes it. Treat others as you would like people to treat you." The Catholic Catechism states: "He who lives by God's merciful love is ready to respond to the Lord's call: 'Go; first be reconciled to your brother'" (CCC Part 2, Section 2, Chapter 2:1424).

Peace

Catholics believe that when people forgive one another, the result will be peace and goodwill between all. Reconciling conflict through negotiation and peaceful means is important to Catholics. The Catechism says: "By recalling the commandment, 'You shall not kill,' our Lord asked for peace of heart and denounced murderous anger and hatred as immoral. *Anger* is a desire for revenge. 'To desire vengeance in order to do evil to someone who should be punished is illicit,' but it is praiseworthy to impose restitution 'to correct vices and maintain justice.' If anger reaches the point of a deliberate desire to kill or seriously wound a neighbor, it is gravely against charity; it is a mortal sin. The Lord says, 'Everyone who is angry with his brother shall be liable to judgment' (2302). Respect for and development of human life require peace. Peace is not merely the absence of war, and it is not limited to maintaining a balance of powers between adversaries. Peace cannot be attained on earth without safeguarding the goods of persons, free communication among men, respect for the dignity of persons and peoples, and the assiduous practice of fraternity. Peace is 'the tranquility of order.' Peace is the work of justice and the effect of charity. Earthly peace is the image and fruit of the *peace of Christ*, the messianic 'Prince of Peace'..." (2304-2305) (CCC Part 3, Section 2, Chapter 2).

Faithfulness

Catholics value relationships that are based on trust and loyalty, especially as this applies to marital fidelity (see the sacrament of matrimony above), but also in relationships with other family members, friends, and co-workers more generally. Being faithful means doing what one says one will do, i.e., being responsible for tasks that are entrusted. Catholics believe this includes being faithful to Jesus Christ, to the Catholic Church, and to their duties in the Church. For this reason, members of the Catholic Church are called "Christ's faithful" (CCC Part 1, Section 2, Chapter 3:871-873).

Honesty and Integrity

Finally, Catholics value being truthful, not holding secrets that might harm the other persons or relationships, and not saying hurtful things about others behind their backs. This applies to institutions as well as individuals. This belief flows naturally from the second Great

Commandment to love neighbor as self and to treat others as one wishes to be treated (see love and compassion above).

CHAPTER 5
CATHOLICISM AND MENTAL HEALTH
Speculations

I now speculate on how Catholic beliefs, practices, and values might influence mental health, either in a positive way or a negative way. The next chapter will put these hypotheses to the test based on systematic research.

Positive Effects on Mental Health

Catholic beliefs, practices and values (BPV), when seriously held and engaged in, have the potential to enhance mental health and increase emotional resiliency. Belief in salvation, in the forgiveness of sins (through the death and resurrection of Jesus Christ), in the meaning of life, and in the existence of life after death – all should help Catholics deal with guilt and provide hope. The emphasis on God's love, compassion, and mercy should help to relieve loneliness, isolation, or the belief that no-one cares. Catholic BPV should help Catholics cope better with loss, change, and difficult life events, and prevent or relieve depression. Belonging to a community of people with a common belief system, common religious practices, and a common emphasis on love of neighbor, might also result in greater social support and stronger, more durable relationships. Jesus, Mary, and the Saints serve as prosocial role models that can be emulated, potentially influencing individual and community well-being.

Religious activities such as praying, saying the rosary, lighting candles, wearing a cross or medal blessed by a priest, or going on religious pilgrimages, may help some Catholics cope with grief and other forms of suffering. The Catholic sacraments provide powerful rituals that may enhance self-esteem and give Catholics activities that enable them to gain control over their lives. Baptism and confirmation mark the Catholic as a member of a spiritual group started by and dedicated to Jesus, the savior of all humanity, whom they believe is God incarnate. Participating in the sacraments of penance and the Eucharist (taking Holy Communion) are activities that Catholics believe purify them from sin and prepare them for heaven, thus providing a sense of peace and security. This is especially true for the act of confession. Being able to unburden oneself in a completely anonymous setting, similar to what occurs during psychotherapy, can have immense benefits – especially when so readily available and free of charge.

Given the sacred nature of the sacrament of matrimony, Catholics may be less likely to separate, divorce, or commit adultery, thus increasing the likelihood that they will have an intact family over their lifetime. This means having a committed spouse available to help cope with stress, and having spouse/children available to provide care during later life when health may decline, thus impacting physical and psychological health. Finally, when Catholics or family members are physically ill, the sacrament of the Anointing of the Sick can provide great comfort and hope for healing. These sacraments and rituals provide continuity to the lives of Catholics, connecting them to the generations that came before them and to the generations that will come after them.

Strong values concerning the need to address social problems, the importance of service, care for the poor and needy, compassion, justice, and emphasis on forgiveness and reconciliation, should give meaning, purpose, and direction to Catholics' daily lives and reduce anger and conflict. Greater meaning and purpose should help counteract feelings of worthlessness and helplessness, and increase motivation towards positive goals. Less anger and conflict should help to reduce social problems among Catholics and prevent the dire consequences of seeking retribution that may include incarceration and deep-seeded resentments that are fertile ground for psychopathology. Other Catholic values that may impact mental health include the importance of being honest and having integrity, which are essential ingredients for success in business and social relationships more generally.

Harold G. Koenig, M.D.

Finally, as noted above, one of the most important Catholic values is respect for human life, especially with regard to committing suicide. The belief that suicide is a mortal sin may prevent some Catholics from doing it, even when suffering is severe. Catholics believe in a Savior who has suffered for them and someone they can emulate. This may provide suffering with meaning that transcends the pain.

Much more controversial, but also directly related to mental health, is the practice of *exorcism*. Little known is the fact that every Catholic diocese today is required to have a specially-trained priest who can perform exorcisms (the casting out demon/demons from those believed to be possessed). For a comprehensive discussion of this issue from a mental health perspective, see the discussion by psychiatrists Pattison and Wintrob (1981). Note that Church leaders have made clear that demonic possession is very rare and most cases after being properly investigated turn out to have mental illness (Squires, 2014). Although highly frowned on by mental health professionals (Karanci, 2014; Scrutton, 2015), reports on the mental health benefits of exorcism in some cases of dissociative identity disorder have been reported (Khan & Sahni, 2013; Irmak, 2014). One mechanism is that exorcism may produce abreaction from hypnotic suggestion. For a relatively recent review that balances risks and benefits of this practice, see Sanford (2016).

The psychological benefits discussed above would be expected among actively practicing Catholics, but not necessarily for nominal or cultural Catholics uninvolved in their faith tradition. According to the Pew Research Center (2015a) and General Social Surveys (Grant, 2014), of persons raised Catholic in the U.S., only 59-65% identify themselves as Catholics when adults (compared to 85% in the 1970s). Even among those who identify as Catholic, more than half don't attend Mass more than once a year, indicating that only about one-third of Catholics overall are active in their faith (Grant, 2014).

Negative Effects on Mental Health

The Catholic Church has many rules and obligations that Catholics are expected to abide by. This together with the fact that many Catholics do not always comply with Church doctrine, leaves plenty of opportunity for guilt. Guilt may in turn increase vulnerability to depression, anxiety, or other emotional problems. Belief that one must suffer in Purgatory for imperfections in this life or be sent to Hell for all of eternity may lead to fear and anxiety, especially when Catholics become sick or approach death as they grow older. In addition, the Catholic values discussed above set the bar high in terms of what Catholics may expect of themselves, leading to psychological strains from failure to live up to these high standards and leading to a lowering of self-esteem.

Catholic rituals and practices may also foster religious obsessions and compulsions among those who are vulnerable to such tendencies. Prayer, saying the rosary, going to confession, or attending Mass may be done out of a compulsion to compensate for obsessive thoughts of sinfulness or impurity. Such individuals may even be viewed by other church members as particularly holy and faithful, rather than as neurotic and needing professional help.

Unrealistic expectations for physical healing from the sacraments (Anointing of the Sick, in particular) or from going on pilgrimage to a Catholic shrine (i.e., Lourdes, Medjugorje, etc.) may lead to disappointment, discouragement, and giving up, exacerbating emotional distress.

Thus, there are many aspects of the Catholic faith that could foster mental illness, not lead to its relief. Consider what Hailparn and Hailparn (1994) say in the *Journal of Contemporary Psychotherapy* about treating Catholic patients:

"Issues such as shame, guilt, masochism, anger, sex, and magical thinking, take on a unique significance when applied to Catholic patients. These issues are a constant struggle for the Catholic because they represent 'mortal sins.' Committing these sins will result, in the patient's mind, in spending an eternity in the tortures of Hell unless they can be erased by confession and appropriate penance. The therapist must actively work to 'exorcise' this punitive superego in a way that may differ from psychotherapy with other patients." (p. 271)

These authors also state (although with little evidence to back up their claim) that Catholics suffer from "powerful superego guilt" that is punitive and demanding, more so than do Protestants. Before such conclusions can be made, however, direction of causation must be considered. Since religious participation and affiliation is voluntary, people self-select themselves into various religious groups. Thus, there may be those with emotional or mental illness due to developmental or genetic reasons who also just happen to be Catholic or who become Catholic because they feel comfortable in this faith tradition (or have had positive experiences with Catholics who have tried to help them, given the strong outreach of Catholics to the mentally ill). Sorting out the chicken from the egg, then, may be a challenge in some cases.

CHAPTER 6
CATHOLICISM AND MENTAL HEALTH
The Research

Rather than relying on public opinion or conventional lore, systematic research may help address questions regarding the benefits vs. the risks of Catholic beliefs and practices. Although research on religion and mental health in Christians of all persuasions has been systematically reviewed elsewhere (Koenig, 2017), a few selected studies will be examined here to illustrate what has been reported when Catholics are compared to non-Catholics. Since there is a wide range of devoutness among Catholics (i.e., only one-third of Catholics in the U.S. are religiously active based on the figures reported earlier), the findings reported here should be interpreted in that light. Where available, then, research on level of religious devoutness and mental health in Catholics will also be examined. Presented now are studies on depression, suicide, general anxiety, guilt, obsessive/compulsive symptoms, and overall well-being.

Depression
Are Catholics more likely than non-Catholics to experience depression? The research findings are equivocal. In a 3-year longitudinal study of 2,812 older adults in New Haven, CT, Idler and Kasl (1992) reported that Catholics were more likely to develop depression than Jews. In contrast, a 2-year longitudinal study of 1,855 older adults in New York City found that Catholics were less likely than Jews to be depressed at baseline and were less likely to become depressed over time (Kennedy et al., 1996). Likewise, in a

10-year longitudinal study of 60 mothers and 151 offspring in New York City, Miller and colleagues (1997) found that Catholic mothers (compared to non-Catholic mothers) were at an 80% lower risk of major depressive disorder at baseline and an 85% lower risk at follow-up. Furthermore, their offspring were at lower risk for depressive disorder as well.

In another report from Miller and colleagues (2012), participants in the above study were followed up 10-years after the initial longitudinal study. They examined 114 offspring (mean age 29 years) of depressed and non-depressed parents, finding no significant difference in depression risk between Catholics and Protestants. However, offspring who indicated that religion/spirituality was very important to them were 76% less likely to develop major depressive disorder during the 10-year follow-up (OR=0.24, 95% CI=0.06-0.95).

Finally, in a 12-year longitudinal study of 48,984 women, weekly attendance predicted less depression in both Catholics and Protestant, with few differences (Li et al, 2016). Thus, based on these selected studies, there is little evidence that Catholics experience more depression than other groups. The conclusion from an earlier systematic review of this topic, then, seems as true today as well as when first reported (McCullough & Larson, 1999): "if there is any relationship between Catholicism and depression, this association is probably too trivial and elusive to merit any serious expenditure of money, time, and effort" (p 128). What is more important than just being Catholic is the extent to which Catholics are actively involved in their religious faith.

Suicide

Durkheim (1897) reported that regions of Europe where Catholics predominated had much lower suicide rates than Protestant areas. He attributed this finding to greater social control, integration and cohesion among Catholics, compared to Protestant who were more independent and free thinking. However, this claim of lower suicide rates in Catholics was challenged because the differences in suicide rate were based on ecological data (Van Poppel & Day, 1996; Stack, 2000). Other researchers have reported a decrease in denominational differences in suicide rate between Catholics and Protestants since World War II due to increases in education (Pyle, 2006).

Nevertheless, recent studies in Europe and the U.S. suggest that differences in suicide between Catholics and Protestants remain significant (Torgler & Schaltegger, 2014; VanderWeele et al., 2016). In Europe, Torgler & Schaltegger (2014) explained that the lower suicide rate in Catholics was largely due to greater belief that suicide is never acceptable. They also found that frequency of religious attendance and time spent with other church members, however, predicted negative attitudes toward suicide among Protestants. Since church attendance is higher in Catholics than Protestants, this may at least partly explained the difference in suicide rate reported by these investigators.

In the most recent report, a 14-year longitudinal study of 89,708 women in the U.S. Nurses' Health Study conducted by the Harvard School of Public Health, investigators found that those who attended religious services at least once per week were 84% less likely to commit suicide compared to women who never attended services (HR=0.16, 95% CI=0.06-0.46) (VanderWeele et al., 2016). There was more than a five-fold reduction in incidence rate from 7 per 100,000 person-years to only 1 per 100,000 person-years. No significant difference overall in suicide rates was found between Catholics (1.5 per 100,000 person-years) and Protestants (2.6 per 100,000 person-years). Effects of religious attendance on suicide rate, however, were particularly strong among Catholics (HR = 0.05, 95% CI = 0.006-0.48), where the effect was 7 times stronger than in Protestants (HR=0.34, 95% CI, 0.10-1.10). Thus, the difference between Catholics and Protestants on suicide rate must be due to more than just frequency of religious attendance. Both the authors of this study and an editorial commentary (Koenig, 2016) suggested that this may be due to Catholic prohibitions against suicide as Torgler & Schaltegger (2014) had suggested earlier.

Anxiety

In one of the first studies to compare Catholics and Protestants on levels of anxiety, Templer and Dotson (1970) found no difference in death anxiety scores between members of these faith groups in Kentucky college students. Likewise, Cohen and colleagues (2005) found no difference on death anxiety between Catholics and Protestants in a sample of 375 adolescents and young adults in New Jersey and Pennsylvania, although an inverse relationship between intrinsic religiosity and death anxiety was stronger in Protestants than in Catholics. Other studies have also found few differences between Catholics and Protestants in fear of death (Ellis et al., 2013).

In a study of 1,058 adults from North Carolina (108 Catholics, 188 Jews, 762 Protestants), Cohen and Hall (2009) found that Catholics and Protestants reported more fear of God ("I worry that God is upset with me") than Jews. In that study, Jews were significantly less religious than Catholics and Protestants, which might have accounted for the difference in worrying that God was upset with them. Jews, however, reported the most death anxiety, Protestants the least, and Catholics were in the middle.

Finally, in a study of 167 German breast cancer patients, Catholics scored significantly lower than Protestants on anxiety assessed using the Hospital Depression & Anxiety Scale (uncontrolled analyses) (Zwingmann et al., 2008). Thus, as for depression, differences in anxiety between Catholics and other religious groups appear to be few or equivocal based on the studies above.

Guilt

Conventional thought (or lore) is that Catholics experience more guilt than others. In fact, a recent *New York Times* article, written near the time of Pope Frances visit to the U.S., was titled "The End of Catholic Guilt" (Egan, 2016). The guilt stereotype for Catholics is also a well-known phenomenon in the clinical literature (Tangney & Dearing, 2002). Given this view of Catholics and the undeniable fact that there are many opportunities for Catholics to feel guilty (as noted above), do Catholics really experience more guilt than members of other religious groups? What do objective comparisons show?

In one of the first studies to quantitatively measure guilt in Catholics and compare it to guilt in members of other faith traditions, London and colleagues (1964) surveyed a small sample of 63 college students in Illinois (15 Catholics, 26 Protestants, 22 Jews). Catholics had the most intensive religious education and Protestants had the least. Jews scored significantly higher on guilt feelings compared to Protestants (3.8 vs. 3.5, p<0.05), although Catholics (3.7) did not significantly differ from Protestants or Jews.

In a larger sample of 281 adults in New York state (average age 46 years), Demaria and Kassinove (1988) compared guilt levels across denomination using a standard 22-item multi-dimensional measure of guilt (interpersonal harm guilt, norm violation guilt, self-control failure guilt). There were 96 Catholics, 46 Protestants, 86 Jews, and 53 non-affiliates in the sample. While investigators found no significant difference in overall guilt between the four groups, Catholics scored significantly higher on "self-control failure" guilt than non-affiliates. The difference, however, was small (11.5 vs. 10.1, $p < 0.05$). Overall religiosity (assessed by the Rohrbaugh & Jessor scale) was positively correlated with overall guilt ($r=0.20$, $p=0.01$), whereas "rationality" was inversely correlated with guilt ($r=-0.51$, $p < 0.001$).

In a much larger sample of 1409 Catholic and 1261 Protestant undergraduate students at the University of Missouri, Sheldon (2006) also reported that Catholics scored higher on introjected motivation (a construct similar to guilt) compared to Protestants. The findings were replicated in a small sample of 40 Catholic, 30 Baptist, and 45 Unitarian adults from the community, helping to confirm the Catholic guilt stereotype. Nevertheless, because of scores on "identified motivation" and "external motivation," Sheldon concluded that Catholics were not driven by guilt in their religious practices.

More recently, Vaisey and Smith (2008) analyzed data on 3,290 U.S. teenagers ages 13-17 and their parents participating in the National Survey of Youth and Religion (NSYR). The NSYR is a nationally representative sample composed of 24.3% Catholics (similar to the percentage of Catholics in the U.S. population in 2002-2003 when the data were collected). Guilt was assessed with the question: "In the last year, how often, if ever, have you found yourself feeling GUILTY about things in your life?" No evidence was found that Catholic teens were more guilty than other young people in this study ($p=0.44$), nor were Catholics more likely than non-Catholics to say that religion caused or relieved their guilt. Investigators also found no evidence that Catholic teens who went more often to confession did so because they felt guilty, or that Catholics who went to confession felt more religious guilt. However, they did find that Catholic teens who went to confession experienced higher levels of "religious relief" from guilt (which was mediated by importance of religious faith).

Thus, while the Catholic guilt stereotype is reasonable and has some evidence supporting it from regional studies examining convenience samples, data from at least one large national sample did not provide solid support for this hypothesis. Furthermore, even among those studies confirming the Catholic guilt hypothesis, differences between Catholics and others while statistically significant are not large. Finally, guilt is not always bad. There is some evidence that Catholic guilt may actually have prosocial consequences (McKay et al., 2013). Indeed, the absence of guilt has long been known to have its own problems, problem that affect not only the individual but also the community (see McCord & McCord's 1964 study of psychopathy).

Obsessive-Compulsive Disorder

Early studies reported higher OCD symptoms in Catholics who were more religious, but also found fewer religious obsessions and compulsions in highly religious Catholics compared to highly religious Protestants. Measures of OCD symptoms used in these studies, however, may have been contaminated by items assessing traditional religious beliefs and values (Koenig, 2004, pp 89-90).

In a study of 111 members of convents, nunneries, Catholic associations, and college students in Northern Italy, Sica and colleagues (2002) found that those with medium or high religiosity scored higher on anxiety symptoms, depressive symptoms, and obsessiveness (Obsessive Beliefs Questionnaire) (uncontrolled correlations).

Abrahamwitz and colleagues (2002) examined differences between 197 Catholic and Protestant college students on religious obsessions and compulsions using the 77-item Penn Inventory of Scrupulosity (made up of two subscales titled "fear of God" and "fear of sinful thoughts"). They found that religious Protestants scored higher on fear of sinful thoughts than religious Catholics, Jews overall, and less religious Protestants. However, in an online survey of 102 Catholic (average age 36 years) and 128 Protestant adults (average age 39), no differences on any aspects of scrupulosity, mental contamination, thought-action fusion, or OCD symptoms were found between the two groups (Fergus, 2014).

Thus, based on these few studies, there is little evidence that Catholics are more prone to OCD symptoms compared to Protestants, and when differences are found, these may be due to the use of measures contaminated by conservative religious beliefs or values.

Psychological Well-being

In an early study of 183 retired Catholic sisters, who were compared with 653 retired older adults from various medical and community settings in the Midwestern U.S., the Catholic sisters had the highest well-being of all groups studied (Koenig et al., 1988; Kvale et al., 1989). In the Cohen and Hall (2009) study described earlier, which took place in predominantly Protestant central North Carolina, Catholics and Jews were not significantly different in overall well-being, but Protestants showed significantly higher well-being (morale) than either Jews or Catholics. Concerning satisfaction with social relationships, Catholics did not differ from either Jews or Protestants, although Protestants reported greater social satisfaction than did Jews. Religiosity (measured by a single self-rated item) was positively correlated with well-being in Protestants but not in Jews or in Catholics (although the correlation in Catholics was similar to that in Protestants, i.e., $r=0.07$ vs. $r=0.11$).

Most recently, Dilmaghani (2017) analyzed data from the Ethnic Diversity Survey of Statistics Canada, a random national sample of 41,695 adults (42% Catholic, 27% Protestant, 16% none, <2% Judaism and Islam). She found that average well-being on a 0 to 5 scale was similar among Catholics (4.3), Protestants (4.8), Jews (4.2), Muslims (4.2), and "none" (4.1). Likewise, the percentage of those who indicated they were "very satisfied" with life was similar in Catholics (48.9%), Protestants (49.2%), Jews (42.8%), Muslims (48.0%), and greater than that in those with no religious affiliation (36.9%). In multivariate models, the particular religious affiliation (Catholic, Protestant, etc.) did not predict life satisfaction once demographic characteristics and religious activity (importance of religion, private religious activities, and religious attendance) were controlled for. Greater religious involvement overall, however, was related to greater well-being, an effect that was equally strong in Catholics and Protestants. Thus, Catholics tend to have similar psychological well-being compared to members of other religious groups, particularly those who are highly religious.

Summary

With the possible exception of experiencing more guilt, Catholics as a group tend to be similar to members of other religious groups in terms of depressive symptoms, suicide, anxiety, obsessions and compulsions, and satisfaction with life, based largely on studies conducted in North America. More important than simply being Catholic, however, is level of Catholic belief, practice, and commitment, which tends to be related to better mental health and greater well-being.

CHAPTER 7
CLINICAL APPLICATIONS

What, then, are the implications for mental health professionals and clergy who are seeking to help Catholic clients or members of a Catholic congregation? The following recommendations for application are based on the existing research, clinical experience, and common sense. We begin with a real life case vignette[1] that illustrates some of the issues that may be encountered with Catholics and how a clinician might respond.

Case Vignette

Mr. T is a 42 year old married Catholic with a long history of alcohol abuse, who developed severe anxiety and depression following a recent diagnosis of lymphoma. While the oncologist had told him that his prognosis for long-term survival was good with treatment, the news hit him hard. He realized that death was possibly in his near future, and he was not ready to go. His wife and son encouraged him to seek help from a psychiatrist. The psychiatrist placed him on antidepressant therapy, and encouraged him to stop drinking, which he did. Despite taking therapeutic doses of antidepressants for months, Mr. T experienced little relief. In fact, his symptoms worsened. As a

---

[1] Details have been altered to protect the person's identity

result, he underwent a series of electroconvulsive treatments (ECT). The ECT treatments produced temporary relief, but the anxiety and depression soon returned, so his psychiatrist referred him to a counselor who might help him with the underlying issues that were driving his emotional symptoms.

One day after several weeks of therapy, his wife called Mr. T's therapist (a non-Catholic) and asked him to talk with Mr. T about a large donation he had recently made to the Catholic Church without telling her. The amount was much more than they could afford, given the bills accumulating from his healthcare. She also mentioned that he was going to confession as often as twice a month and attending Mass several times per week. When questioned by the therapist about the donation and increased religious activity, Mr. T asked: "Do you know what *restitution* means? I've done some bad things in my life." When encouraged to elaborate, Mr. T slowly and tearfully revealed: "I've been cheating customers in my business. I cheated on my wife over and over again for years. The woman I had the affair with got pregnant and I forced her to have an abortion. I need restitution." The therapist urged him to continue. "I'm afraid I'm going to Hell. The donation will help to pay off some of my sins." When asked about his increased religious activity, Mr. T said "Going to confession and Mass give me some relief."

After listening to Mr. T, the therapist gently suggested he see a Catholic priest with mental health training to discuss his concerns. Mr. T agreed to see a Catholic pastoral counselor, who helped him understand the present day teachings of the Catholic Church a little better. After several months of counseling and continued medication therapy, Mr. T's anxiety slowly improved and his religious activities normalized.

One in five patients seen by mental health professionals in the U.S. will be Catholic and many will be active in their religious faith. How can knowledge about the beliefs, practices, and values of Catholics, along with information gathered from systematic research, assist clinicians when treating Catholic patients? The following are recommendations for mental health professionals and clergy who might be called on to provide counsel to Catholics.

(1) <u>Take a Spiritual History</u>. Find out how active the person is in their faith community and how important being Catholic is to them. If previously involved in the Catholic Church, but now no longer active, gently explore this. Determine if they were raised Catholic or have converted to Catholicism. If raised Catholic, ask whether their Catholic upbringing was a positive or negative experience. Ask how important Catholicism is to their parents, and whether this was also true during the client's childhood. If a convert to Catholicism, ask what led up to the conversion. Ask about specific religious practices now engaged in, such as how often they attend Mass, participate in other social Catholic functions, go to confession, pray, say the rosary, fast, or have pictures or statues of Jesus, Mary, or Saints in their home. Ask about any positive or negative experiences concerning their Catholic faith or interactions with Catholic clergy. Ask how important it is for them to follow Catholic teachings.

(2) <u>Support for Therapy/Treatment</u>. Ask clients if members of their family or support group are Catholic and how active they are. Are there any strong opinions among persons who are close them about their decision to receive counseling? This will provide information about whether progress made in therapy will be supported or resisted outside the therapist's office.

(3) <u>Safe Place</u>. Provide a friendly and safe place where clients can talk freely about their religious faith, good or bad, without judgment. Maintain a respectful, interested, and receptive attitude at all times to the client's Catholic faith (whether the person is currently active or not, whether he or she speaks well of it or not).

(4) <u>Confession</u>. If clients have gone to confession, ask about what the experience was like for them, and whether it was helpful. If the client has not gone to confession lately, gently explore why not without implying that they should have gone or should go in the future.

(5) <u>Role in Current Problem</u>. Determine what role their Catholic faith may be playing in the current problem that help is being sought for. If they have trouble answering this question, ask them to think

about it and then raise the question again during a subsequent visit. Obtaining collateral information from family members may also be useful.

(6) <u>Guilt</u>. Listen for feelings of excessive guilt over real or imagined transgressions. Don't try to immediately rationalize or remove the guilt; rather, seek to understand it better from the client's faith perspective. Identify core beliefs that may be driving the guilt, but be careful in overtly challenging religious beliefs. It may be necessary to seek counsel from Catholic clergy or even to arrange co-therapy with a Catholic pastoral counselor (as in the case above).

(7) <u>Challenge/Re-educate</u>. Regardless of Hailparn and Hailparn's (1994) suggestion to "exorcise" the "punitive superego" of Catholics, don't be too ready to do this. After a solid therapeutic relationship has been established and a safe space created, the gentle challenge of harshly punitive core beliefs may be indicated and necessary. As noted above, it may be best to wait until obtaining consultation with a mental health or religious professional who is knowledgeable about the Catholic tradition. Re-education regarding religion should probably only be done by someone whom the client views as an authority in the Catholic faith. Of course, non-Catholic therapists can always use gentle "Socratic questioning" that gently imply that beliefs or practices may not be consistent with mainstream Catholic theology and therefore be contributing unnecessarily to the person's distress.

(8) <u>Role of the Sacraments</u>. In addition to possibly recommending confession (if this has not already been tried), for devout Catholics with serious mental illness, the mental health professional may consider suggesting they see a Catholic priest to administer the sacrament of the "Anointing of the Sick" (see discussion above). Although such a suggestion is admittedly controversial, since little or no research exists that might indicate benefit, this recommendation may be reasonable in some cases depending on the patient and the openness of the Catholic priest whom he or she is being referred to. Even more caution should be displayed before suggesting that a devout Catholic with serious mental illness see a priest for the rite of exorcism (see discussion above). This should only be considered for

someone with dissociative identity disorder, and even with this disorder, there is no good data to support its use. Exorcism for psychotic illnesses such as schizophrenia does not help (personal communication William P. Wilson, M.D., Duke University professor emeritus of psychiatry).

(9) <u>Support Beliefs/Practices</u>. Don't be too reluctant to support the Catholic religious beliefs or practices that the client finds helpful (or might find helpful in the future as a way of coping with emotional issues), but do so from the client's perspective. If the client is receptive and open to healthy religious practices, then these may be encouraged; if the client shows resistance, don't push too heard. However, it may be informative to gently explore where the resistance is coming from at a future session. Never give clients the impression that they are not religious enough, since they probably get plenty of that from family and fellow church members. Whether it is a psychiatrist prescribing biological therapies or a therapist providing counseling, the mental health professional should be viewed by the client as neutral, interested in, open to, and supportive of the client's Catholic faith, but always on the client's side and never judgmental. The same applies to Catholic clergy who are counseling members of their congregation.

CHAPTER 8
CATHOLIC RESPONSE TO MENTAL ILLNESS

As noted above, Catholics come from a particular social culture and value system. Catholic beliefs that promote compassion and love of neighbor, particularly to those who are less fortunate, should influence attitudes toward those with mental illness. Back in the 5th century AD, St. Augustine wrote the following:

> "Crazy people say and do many incongruous things, things for the most part alien to their intentions and their characters, certainly contrary to their good intentions and characters; and when we think about their words and actions, or see them with our eyes, we can scarcely — or possibly we cannot at all — restrain our tears, if we consider their situation as it deserves to be considered." (St. Augustine, City of God, 413AD, translation by Bettenson, 2003, p 465)

It should not be surprising, then, that the Catholic Church founded one of the first mental hospitals for care of the mentally ill in 490 AD in Jerusalem (Alexander & Selesnick, 1966). In the 6th century, the Church cared for the mentally ill in monasteries (Fleming, 1929). The first psychiatric hospital in Europe, the Pryor of St. Mary's of Bethlehem, was established by the Church in London in 1247. The latter hospital was later replaced by Bethlehem Hospital or Bethlem, which remains there today as the Bethlem Royal Hospital (Andrews et al., 1997).

Admittedly, the Catholic Church was anything but compassionate to the mentally at different times in history, particularly during the Middle Ages. As the number of people with mental illness grew in Europe, there was pressure on ecclesiastical authorities to do something, leading to the view that mental illness was caused by demonic possession. The Inquisition was established in 1233, and *Malleus Maleficarum* (guide for the treatment of the possessed) was published in 1487. This was followed by a wave of persecution that would lead to the death of thousands of mentally ill people who were burned at the stake or decapitated during the next 200 years (Zilboorg, 1941). In the famous Salem Witch Trials in 1692 in New England, nearly 100 people would be accused and 19 executed for being witches or demon possessed (Gamwell & Tomes, 1995). Much has changed, though, since then.

The Catholic Church today has some of the largest programs proving social services to the mentally ill in the U.S. and around the world (Koenig, 2004, pp 193-194). Catholic Charities in the U.S. had its origins in 1727 when French nuns established an orphanage in New Orleans. Today it serves approximately seven million people each year by providing disaster assistance, emergency financial aid, food services, health clinics, housing services, and mental health counseling (Hoover, 2016). In addition, there are a number of Catholic psychiatric hospitals (Saint Luke's Institute in Silver Spring, Maryland, for example), psychiatric inpatient wards at Catholic hospitals, residential treatment facilities, and outpatient mental health centers throughout the U.S. Caritas International advocates for those with mental health problems around the world (Caritas, 2017).

CHAPTER 9
SUMMARY AND CONCLUSIONS

Catholics are members of a faith tradition and institution that dates back over 2,000 years. The religious beliefs, practices, and social values professed by the Catholic Church are very important to some Catholics, not important to others, and inconsistently and ambivalently held by yet others. Knowing something about Catholicism is necessary for mental health professionals to provide holistic, respectful and sensitive care to Catholic clients. Every Catholic is unique in the particular combination of religious beliefs, practices, and values that he or she holds dear.

Catholics in general have mental health that is comparable to members of other faith traditions, and greater religious involvement is related to better mental health in most cases (as is true for Christians in general). The Catholic Church places many obligations and rules on the faithful, and promises harsh consequences in the hereafter for those who fail to comply. While this may increase feelings of guilt among Catholics who see themselves as not living up to these high expectations, particularly those who are vulnerable to such anxieties, the current research suggests that guilt in Catholics may not be nearly as serious a problem as some have assumed.

There are many applications to clinical practice that follow from the information presented in this chapter, especially in terms of taking a careful and detailed spiritual history. Finally, Catholics have a long tradition of compassion for the less fortunate, and that includes those with mental illness or emotional problems. Mental health professionals and clergy should find solid partners among Catholic religious and social service professionals as they pursue goals that are common to all.

REFERENCES

Abramowitz J, Huppert J, Cohen A, Tolin D, Cahill S (2002). Religious obsessions and compulsions in a non-clinical sample: The Penn Inventory of Scrupulosity (PIOS). *Behaviour Research and Therapy* 40:825–838.

Alexander, F.G., & Selesnick, S.T. (1966). *The History of Psychiatry: An Evaluation of Psychiatric Thought and Practice from Prehistoric Times to the Present.* New York: New American Library, Inc.

Andrews J, Briggs A, Porter R, Tucker P, Waddington K (1997). *The History of Bethlem.* New York, NY: Routledge

Annuarium Statisticum Ecclesiae (2016). *Pontifical Yearbook 2016 and the Annuarium Statisticum Ecclesiae 2014: Dynamics of a Church in Transformation.* Retrieved from https://press.vatican.va/content/salastampa/en/bollettino/pubblico/2016/03/05/160305b.html (accessed on 1/2/17)

Awad, G. A., & Saunders, E. B. (1991). Male adolescent sexual assaulters clinical observations. *Journal of Interpersonal Violence, 6*(4), 446-460.

Barrett WP (2016). The largest U.S. charities for 2016. *Forbes Magazine*, Dec 14. Retrieved from http://www.forbes.com/sites/williampbarrett/2016/12/14/the-largest-u-s-charities-for-2016/#8b95de9267d9 (accessed on 1/9/17)

Berry E.S. (2009). *The Church of Christ: An Apologetic and Dogmatic Treatise.* Eugene, OR: Wipf and Stock Publishers

Bettenson H (translator) (2003). *The City of God (by St. Augustine, Bishop of Hippo).* London, England: Penguin Classics

CARA (2008). Sacraments today: Belief and practice among U.S. Catholics. Washington DC: Center for Applied Research in the Apostolate at Georgetown University. Retrieved from http://webcache.googleusercontent.com/search?q=cache:ZsvH9vhF e5kJ:cara.georgetown.edu/sacramentsesum.pdf+&cd=9&hl=en&ct= clnk&gl=us (accessed on 1/9/17)

Caritas (2017). Mental health. *Caritas International.* Retrieved from http://www.caritas.org/?s=mental+health (accessed on 1/10/17)

Catechism of the Catholic Church (1993). *Libreria Editrice Vaticana, Citta del Vaticano.* Retrieved from http://www.vatican.va/archive/ENG0015/_INDEX.HTM (accessed on 1/7/17)

Catholic Catechist (2016). Catholic values today. *Catholic Catechist: Providing Resources to Religious Educators.* Retrieved from http://www.catholiccatechist.org/freeFiles/239_Catholic_Values_T oday_Handout.doc (accessed on 1/10/17).

Code of Canon Law (1983). Book II, Part 1, Title I. The obligations and rights of all the Christian faithful, line 222. *Libreria Editrice Vaticana, Citta del Vaticano.* Retrieved from http://www.vatican.va/archive/ENG1104/_PU.HTM (accessed 1/9/17)

Cohen, A. B., & Hall, D. E. (2009). Existential beliefs, social satisfaction, and well-being among Catholic, Jewish, and Protestant older adults. *International Journal for the Psychology of Religion, 19*(1), 39-54.

Cohen, A. B., Pierce, J. D., Chambers, J., Meade, R., Gorvine, B. J., & Koenig, H. G. (2005). Intrinsic and extrinsic religiosity, belief in the afterlife, death anxiety, and life satisfaction in young Catholics and Protestants. *Journal of Research in Personality, 39*(3), 307-324.

CSS (2016). Catholic Social Services: Reaching out, healing lives. Retrieved from http://www.cssdioc.org/index.html (accessed on 1/10/17).

Demaria, T., & Kassinove, H. (1988). Predicting guilt from irrational beliefs, religious affiliation and religiosity. *Journal of Rational Emotive and Cognitive Behavior Therapy, 6*(4), 259-272.

Dilmaghani, M. (2017). Religiosity and subjective well-being in Canada. *Journal of Happiness Studies*, Jan 3, E-pub ahead of print.

Doughty, S. (2015). Catholics can now remarry after they are divorced, senior cardinals say... but only if they abstain from sex. *Daily Mail*, September 10. Retrieved from http://www.dailymail.co.uk/news/article-3230133/Catholics-remarry-divorced-senior-cardinals-say-abstain-sex.html (accessed on 1/7/17)

Durkheim, E. (1897). *Le Suicide*. Paris: F. Alcan

Egan, T. (2016). The end of Catholic guilt. *New York Times*, April 15. Retrieved from https://www.nytimes.com/2016/04/15/opinion/the-end-of-catholic-guilt.html?_r=0 (accessed on 1/14/17).

Ellis, L., Wahab, E. A., & Ratnasingan, M. (2013). Religiosity and fear of death: a three-nation comparison. *Mental Health, Religion & Culture, 16*(2), 179-199.

Fairchild, M (2016). Number of Eastern Orthodox Christians worldwide. *About Religion*, retrieved from http://christianity.about.com/od/easternorthodoxy/p/orthodoxprofile.htm (accessed on 1/2/17)

Fergus, T. A. (2014). Mental contamination and scrupulosity: Evidence of unique associations among Catholics and Protestants. *Journal of Obsessive-Compulsive and Related Disorders, 3*(3), 236-242.

Fleming P (1929). The medical aspects of the medieval monastery in England. *Proceedings of the Royal Society of Medicine* 22:25-36.

Gamwell L, Tomes N (1995). *Madness in America: Cultural and Medical Perceptions of Mental Illness Before 1914.* NY: State University of New York at Binghamton and Cornell University Press.

Geisler, N (1998). Albright, William F. and Archaeology, New Testament and passim. *Baker Encyclopedia of Christian Apologetics.* Ada, MI: Baker Publishing Co.

Grant, T. (2014). Growing divide between 'practicing Catholics' and 'cultural Catholics' in two graphs. *Religion News Service*, Feb 10. Retrieved from http://religionnews.com/2014/02/10/graphs-growing-divide-practicing-catholics-cultural-catholics/ (accessed on 1/12/17)

Gray MM, Gaunt TP, Saunders C (2013). U.S. Catholic online giving. *Center for Applied Research in the Apostolate* (United States Conference of Catholic Bishops). Washington DC: Georgetown University. Retrieved from http://www.usccb.org/about/national-collections/upload/National-Collections-Report-Revised.pdf (accessed on 1/9/17)

Hailparn, D. F., & Hailparn, M. (1994). Treating the Catholic patient: Unique dynamics and implications for psychotherapy. *Journal of Contemporary Psychotherapy, 24*(4), 271-279.

Hoover (2016). Catholic Charities USA company information. Retrieved from http://www.hoovers.com/company-information/cs/company-profile.catholic_charities_usa.3ade393994872f9d.html (accessed on 1/10/17)

Idler, E. L., & Kasl, S. V. (1992). Religion, disability, depression, and the timing of death. *American Journal of Sociology* 97(4):1052-1079.

Irmak, M.K. (2014). Schizophrenia or possession? *Journal of Religion and Health, 53*, 773-777.

John Paul II (1999). *Heaven, Hell and Purgatory.* Retrieved from https://www.ewtn.com/library/PAPALDOC/JP2HEAVN.HTM (accessed on 1/6/17)

Karanci, A.N. (2014). Concerns about schizophrenia or possession? *Journal of Religion and Health, 53*, 1691-92.

Kennedy, G. J., Kelman, H. R., Thomas, C., & Chen, J. (1996). The relation of religious preference and practice to depressive symptoms among 1,855 older adults. *Journal of Gerontology* 51(6): P301-P308.

Khan, I.D. & Sahni, A.K. (2013). Possession at high altitude (4575 m/15000 ft). *Kathmandu University Medical Journal, 11*(3), 253-55.

Koenig HG (2004). *Faith & Mental Health: Religious Resources for Healing.* Philadelphia, PA: Templeton Foundation Press

Koenig HG (2016). Association of religious involvement and suicide. *JAMA Psychiatry* 73(8): 775-776.

Koenig HG (2017). *Christianity and Mental Health.* Amazon: CreatSpace

Koenig HG, Kvale JN, Ferrel C (1988). Religion and well-being in later life. *The Gerontologist* 28:18-28

Kvale JN, Koenig HG, Ferrel C (1989). Life satisfaction of the aging woman religious. *Journal of Religion and Aging* 5(4):68-72

Li, S., Okereke, O. I., Chang, S. C., Kawachi, I., & VanderWeele, T. J. (2016). Religious service attendance and lower depression among women—a prospective cohort study. *Annals of Behavioral Medicine, 50*(6), 876-884.

London, P., Schulman, R. E., & Black, M. S. (1964). Religion, guilt, and ethical standards. *Journal of Social Psychology*, *63*(1), 145-159.

Lumen Gentium (1964). *Dogmatic Constitution on the Church: Lumen Gentium*. Solemnly Promulgated by His Holiness Pope Paul VI, November 21. Retrieved from http://www.vatican.va/archive/hist_councils/ii_vatican_council/documents/vat-ii_const_19641121_lumen-gentium_en.html (accessed on 1/16/17).

Makinen V. (2014). Moral philosophical arguments against suicide in the Middle Ages (pp 129-145). In ML Honkasalo and M Tuominen (eds), *Culture, Suicide, and the Human Condition*. New York, NY: Berghahn Books.

McCord, W., & McCord, J. (1964). *The Psychopath: An Essay on the Criminal Mind*. Princeton: Van Nostrand.

McCullough, M. E., & Larson, D. B. (1999). Religion and depression: a review of the literature. *Twin Research*, *2*(02), 126-136.

McKay, R., Herold, J., & Whitehouse, H. (2013). Catholic guilt? Recall of confession promotes prosocial behavior. *Religion, Brain & Behavior*, *3*(3), 201-209.

Miller L, Wickramaratne P, Gameroff MJ, Sage M, Tenke CE, Weissman MM (2012). Religiosity and major depression in adults at high risk: A ten-year prospective study. *American Journal of Psychiatry* 169(1): 89–94.

Miller, L., Warner, V., Wickramaratne, P., & Weissman, M. (1997). Religiosity and depression: Ten-year follow-up of depressed mothers and offspring. *Journal of the American Academy of Child & Adolescent Psychiatry*, 36(10), 1416-1425.

Mounce, R (1998). *The Book of Revelation. The New International Commentary on the New Testament Series*. Cambridge, UK: Eerdmans.

Norman, E., Barrett, J. (2007). *The Roman Catholic Church an Illustrated History.* Oakland, CA: University of California Press

Pattison, E. M., & Wintrob, R. M. (1981). Possession and exorcism in contemporary America. *Journal of Operational Psychiatry, 12*(1), 13-20.

Pew Research Center (2014). Frequency of prayer among Catholics. *Religious Landscape Study.* Retrieved from http://www.pewforum.org/religious-landscape-study/religious-tradition/catholic/frequency-of-prayer/ (accessed on 1/9/17)

Pew Research Center (2015a). America's changing religious landscape. *Pew Research Center Religion and the Public Life.* Retrieved from http://www.pewforum.org/2015/05/12/americas-changing-religious-landscape/ (accessed on 1/13/17).

Pew Research Center (2015b). Most Catholics regularly receive communion when they attend Mass. *Pew Research Center Religion and the Public Life.* Retrieved from http://www.pewresearch.org/fact-tank/2015/09/24/5-facts-about-communion-and-american-catholics/ft_15-09-17-catholicsmass/ (accessed on 1/8/17)

Pew Research Center (2015c). Key findings about American Catholics. *Pew Research Center Religion and the Public Life.* Retrieved from http://www.pewresearch.org/fact-tank/2015/09/02/key-findings-about-american-catholics/ (accessed on 1/8/17)

Pew Research Center (2016). If the U.S. had 100 people: Charting Americans' religious affiliations. *Pew Research Center Religion and the Public Life.* Retrieved from http://www.pewresearch.org/fact-tank/2016/11/14/if-the-u-s-had-100-people-charting-americans-religious-affiliations/ (accessed on 1/8/17)

Pyle, RE (2006). Trends in religious stratification: Have religious group socioeconomic distinctions declined in recent decades? *Sociology of Religion 671(1):*61–79.

Robinson, JAT (2000). *Redating the New Testament.* Eugene, OR: Wipf & Stock

Sanford, J. R. (2016). Facing our demons: Psychiatric perspectives on exorcism rituals. *The Hilltop Review*, 8(2):87-93

Scrutton, A.P. (2015). Schizophrenia or possession? A reply to Kemal Irmak and Nuray Karanci. *Journal of Religion and Health, 54*, 1963-68.

Sheldon, K. M. (2006). Catholic Guilt? Comparing Catholics' and Protestants' Religious Motivations. *International Journal for the Psychology of Religion*, 16(3), 209-223.

Sica C, Novara C, Sanavio E (2002). Religiousness and obsessive–compulsive cognitions and symptoms in an Italian population. *Behaviour Research and Therapy* 40:813–823.

Squires, N. (2014). Pope Frances praises exorcists for combating 'the Devil's works." *The Telegraph*, Oct 28. Retrieved from http://www.telegraph.co.uk/news/worldnews/the-pope/11193681/Pope-Francis-praises-exorcists-for-combating-the-Devils-works.html (accessed on 1/11/17)

Stack S (2000). Suicide: a 15-year review of the sociological literature: part II: Modernization and social integration perspectives. *Suicide & Life Threatening Behavior* 30(2):163-176.

Srawley JH (1900). *Ignatius Epistle to the Smyrnaeans*. Retrieved from https://en.wikipedia.org/wiki/Catholic_(term)#cite_note-Smyrnaeans_8-13 (accessed on 3/4/17)

Tangney, J.P., & Dearing, R.L. (2002). *Shame and Guilt*. New York, NY: Guilford Press

Templer, D. I., & Dotson, E. (1970). Religious correlates of death anxiety. *Psychological Reports, 26*(3), 895-897.

Torgler, B., & Schaltegger, C. (2014). Suicide and religion: new evidence on the differences between Protestantism and Catholicism. *Journal for the Scientific Study of Religion, 53*(2), 316-340.

United States Conference of Bishops (2017). Fasting & abstinence. Retrieved from http://www.usccb.org/prayer-and-worship/liturgical-year/lent/catholic-information-on-lenten-fast-and-abstinence.cfm (accessed on 1/9/17)

USCCB (2004). The nature and scope of sexual abuse of minors by Catholic priests and deacons in the United States 1950-2002: A research study conducted by the John Jay College of Criminal Justice, the University of New York. Washington, DC: United States Conference of Catholic Bishops. Retrieved from http://www.usccb.org/issues-and-action/child-and-youth-protection/upload/The-Nature-and-Scope-of-Sexual-Abuse-of-Minors-by-Catholic-Priests-and-Deacons-in-the-United-States-1950-2002.pdf (accessed on 1/14/17)

Ut Unum (1995). Ioannes Paulus Pages II Ut Unum Sint on commitment to ecumenism. Retrieved from http://w2.vatican.va/content/john-paul-ii/en/encyclicals/documents/hf_jp-ii_enc_25051995_ut-unum-sint.html (accessed on 1/2/17)

Vaisey, S., & Smith, C. (2008). Catholic guilt among US teenagers: A research note. *Review of Religious Research* 49(4): 415-426.

Van Poppel, F., & Day, L. H. (1996). A test of Durkheim's theory of suicide--without committing the" ecological fallacy". *American Sociological Review*, 500-507.

VanderWeele TJ, Li S, Tsai AC, Kawachi I (2016). Association between religious service attendance and lower suicide rates among US women. *JAMA Psychiatry* 73(8):845-851.

Warren R (2002). *The Purpose Driven Life*. Grand Rapids, MI: Zondervan

Wright B, Roberts E (2017). Australia: 7% of Catholic priests abused children, commission finds. *Cable Network News (CNN)*, Feb 7. Retrieved from http://www.cnn.com/2017/02/06/asia/australia-catholic-sex-abuse/?iid=ob_homepage_deskrecommended_pool (accessed on 2/7/17).

Zenit (2010). Anointing for Mental Disorders. *Zenit Daily Dispatch* (ZENIT International News Agency), Oct 12. Retrieved from http://www.ewtn.com/library/Liturgy/zlitur334.htm (accessed on 1/16/17)

Zilboorg G. (1941). *A History of Medical Psychology*. NY: WW Norton Co.

Zwingmann, C., Müller, C., Körber, J., & Murken, S. (2008). Religious commitment, religious coping and anxiety: a study in German patients with breast cancer. *European Journal of Cancer Care*, *17*(4), 361-370.

ABOUT THE AUTHOR

Harold G. Koenig, M.D., M.H.Sc., completed his undergraduate education at Stanford University, nursing school at San Joaquin Delta College, medical school training at the University of California at San Francisco, and geriatric medicine, psychiatry, and biostatistics training at Duke University Medical Center. He is currently board certified in general psychiatry, and formerly boarded in family medicine, geriatric medicine, and geriatric psychiatry, and is on the faculty at Duke as Professor of Psychiatry and Behavioral Sciences, and Associate Professor of Medicine. He is also Adjunct Professor in the Department of Medicine at King Abdulaziz University, Jeddah, Saudi Arabia, and in the School of Public Health at Ningxia Medical University, Yinchuan, People's Republic of China. Dr. Koenig is Director of the Center for Spirituality, Theology and Health at Duke University Medical Center, and has published extensively in the fields of mental health, geriatrics, and religion, with over 500 scientific peer-reviewed articles and book chapters, and more than 40 books. His research on religion, health and ethical issues in medicine has been featured on dozens of national and international TV news programs (including ABC's World News Tonight, The Today Show, Good Morning America. Dr. Oz Show, and NBC Nightly News), over a hundred national or international radio programs, and hundreds of newspapers and magazines (including Reader's Digest, Parade Magazine, Newsweek, Time, and Guidepost). Dr. Koenig has given testimony before the U.S. Senate (1998) and U.S. House of Representatives (2008) concerning the benefits of religion and spirituality on public health, and travels widely to give seminars and workshops on this topic. He is the recipient of the 2012 Oskar Pfister Award from the American Psychiatric Association.